CRAFT BOX

ANCIENT GREEKS

12 projects to make and do

Published in paperback in 2014 by Wayland
Copyright © Wayland 2014

Wayland
338 Euston Road
London NW1 3BH

Wayland Australia
Level 17/207 Kent Street
Sydney, NSW 2000

Editor: Elizabeth Brent
Designer: Rocket Design (East Anglia) Ltd
Craft stylist: Annalees Lim
Photographer: Simon Pask, N1 Studios

The website addresses (URLs) listed in this book are correct at
the time of going to press. However, it is possible that contents
or addresses may have changed since the publication of this book.
No responsibility for any such changes can be accepted by either
the author or the Publisher.

Picture acknowledgements:
All step-by-step craft photography: Simon Pask, N1 Studios; images
used throughout for creative graphics: Shutterstock.

A cataloguing record for this title is available at the British Library.
Dewey number: 938-dc23

ISBN: 978 0 7502 8404 2

10 9 8 7 6 5 4 3 2 1

Printed in China

Wayland is a division of Hachette Children's Books, an
Hachette UK company.
www.hachette.co.uk

Contents

the Ancient Greeks

The ancient Greeks lived from about 3000–430 BCE

The ancient Greeks lived more than 2000 years ago on the mainland and islands of Greece and in colonies in Europe and North Africa. A farming and seafaring people, they lived in independent city states, trading amongst themselves and the colonies.

Ancient Greek writers and philosophers, such as Plato and Aristotle, developed ideas that still shape the way we think and do things today.

The ancient Greeks enjoyed the arts. They built huge stone theatres for performing and watching plays. Sculptors carved statues and decorated temples such as the Parthenon, built to worship the many gods and goddesses of Greek religion and mythology.

Ancient Greek craftsmen were skilled at working with materials including marble, clay, metals, wood and leather. They were mostly 'free men' who used slaves as assistants, and some came from the colonies, bringing new skills. Their workshops were grouped together in cities, so areas became known for one craft, such as pottery or leather tanning.

Greek buildings and objects, from temples and sculptures to pottery and jewellery, can tell us lots of fascinating facts about life in ancient Greece. They can also inspire you to make some Greek crafts of your own!

make

Theatre masks

The ancient Greeks went to the theatre to watch plays by great playwrights such as Sophocles. Actors wore masks made from wood, linen or leather to show different characters and emotions in comic or tragic dramas.

1 Cut away two foil plates to make two mask shapes.

2 Hold each mask up to your face and mark where to place the eyes and mouth. Draw them on then use the scissors to make holes and cut around the lines. Cover the cut edges with sticky tape.

3 Paint the craft sticks with metallic paint.

4 Cut thin strips of foil or foil chocolate wrappers and glue or tape them onto the mask to make hair or beards.

5 Glue or tape a craft stick onto the back of each mask.

6 Cut thin strips of foil and glue them to the face of each mask to make frown lines. Use glitter glue to draw a nose onto each mask, and to go around the mouth and eyes, exaggerating the happy or sad expression.

Did you know...
There were no women actors so men wore masks to play female parts.

make a
Fish dish

Potters made pots, bowls and dishes of all shapes and sizes for storing and serving food and drinks in ancient Greece. They used red and black clay, decorating it with animals, birds or figures from myths.

You will need:

- ◎ Plain and terracotta air dry clay
- ◎ Rolling pin
- ◎ Clay tools
- ◎ Glue
- ◎ Black paint
- ◎ Brush

1 Take a piece of plain clay and work it with your hands to soften it. Roll it flat then use a clay tool to cut a circle to make a base for the dish.

2 Take a larger piece of plain clay and mould it with your hands to form a shallow dish shape. Shape a dip in the middle of the dish.

3 Roll two pieces of plain clay to form the handles and attach one to each side of the dish.

4

Roll a piece of terracotta clay flat. Use the craft knife to cut out three fish shapes. Cut out eye holes and make small slits along their bodies.

Did you know...
The dip in the middle of fish dishes was for fish sauce or oil.

5

Press the terracotta clay shapes onto the plain clay dish while it is still soft. Allow the clay to air dry.

6

Glue the dish to the base and allow to dry. Paint the whole dish black apart from the terracotta fish.

make a
Medusa headdress

Medusa is one of the most famous characters in Greek mythology. Cursed by the goddess Athena, she had snakes that grew instead of hair, and could turn anyone who looked directly at her into stone.

1 Paint the hair band and the Styrofoam eggs with green acrylic paint and allow to dry. Placing the band and eggs on cocktail sticks stuck into Styrofoam will make this easier.

2 Glue two red sequins or fake gems onto each Styrofoam egg to look like snakes' eyes.

3 Take a pair of pipe cleaners and twist them together. Repeat until you have several snakes.

4 Use the scissors to expose the wires at one end of the pipe cleaners and push each one firmly into a Styrofoam egg.

5 Twist the other end of the snake around the hair band. Repeat with the remaining snakes, working around the band.

6 Wind pipe cleaners around the band to cover any pipe cleaner ends that are showing, folding back and twisting the sharp ends. Use a pencil or your fingers to bend and shape the snakes.

Did you know...
Women in ancient Greece wore head bands made from metal or ribbons.

make an
Olympic torch

The Olympic Games began in ancient Greece over 2700 years ago. They were held in honour of the god Zeus. A torch was lit every four years at the start of the Olympics and burned throughout the Games.

You will need:
◎ Card
◎ Scissors
◎ Gold, yellow or orange wrapping paper
◎ Glue and sticky tape
◎ Punchinella or gold netting
◎ Yellow and red cellophane

1 Cut out a piece of card in the shape of a triangle.

2 Cut out and glue on wrapping paper to cover the triangle.

3 Cut a piece of Punchinella or gold netting and tape it onto the wrapping paper.

4 Roll the triangle into a cone and glue or tape the edges together.

Did you know... Greek Olympic champions were awarded olive wreaths which they wore like crowns.

5 Snip jagged edges into several pieces of red and yellow cellophane, then scrunch them up to form flames.

6 Bunch the cellophane together then glue it around the inside edges of the cone.

make a
Perfume bottle

An aryballos was a small flask used in ancient Greece to hold perfumes or bathing oils. It could be shaped like a globe, a shell, an animal, a face or a foot. Some aryballoi had cords for wearing around the wrist or hanging from wall pegs.

1 Blow up a small, round balloon. Tape a thin strip of card, about 2cm-wide, into a circle to make a base for the bottle.

2 Cut a strip of card 3cm by 12cm and tape it into a circle. Tape it onto the top of the balloon to make the bottle neck.

3 Cut a circle of corrugated card 5cm in diameter. Cut a hole in the middle of it, slightly narrower than the bottle neck. Tape the disc to the bottle neck.

4 To make papier maché, mix equal parts of white glue and water. Dip strips of tissue paper into the glue mix, then smooth them onto the sides of the balloon and card. Finish with a layer of kitchen paper and allow the bottle to dry.

Did you know... Ancient Greek bathers used a 'strigil' or metal scraper to clean their bodies.

5 Paint the bottle and allow it to dry, then decorate it. Look at pictures of Greek aryballoi in books and on the Internet to give you ideas.

6 Cut a piece of cord or ribbon and tie it around the bottle neck.

make a
Golden wreath

The ancient Greeks wore wreaths made from grape vines for the festival of the wine god, Dionysus. Wreaths made from gold were worn for religious ceremonies, left as gifts for the gods at temples and placed in burial tombs.

You will need:
- ◎ Large paper plate
- ◎ Scissors
- ◎ Gold wrapping paper, foil or card
- ◎ Glue
- ◎ Gold sweet wrappers
- ◎ Fine gold craft wire
- ◎ Gold glitter glue

1 Cut the rim off the paper plate to make a base for your wreath. Then cut out a short section and snip the ends into points.

2 Cut out vine leaves of different sizes from gold foil, card or wrapping paper.

3 Fold the leaves in half, and open them out again.

4 Glue the leaves onto the rim base, facing in different directions. The leaves on the right side of the wreath should point towards the right end, the leaves on the left should point to the left end.

Did you know...
The Greeks wore wreaths made from myrtle leaves for weddings and feasts.

5 Scrunch small pieces of gold foil or sweet wrappers into balls. Cut short lengths of craft wire and wind each piece around two or three gold balls, leaving a long end free.

6 Wind the end of each piece of wire around the wreath base and glue on more leaves to hide the wire. Decorate your wreath with glitter glue.

make a Fibula

In ancient Greece, men and women wore simple tunics called chitons made from linen. The tunics were pinned at the shoulders with a pin or brooch called a fibula.

1 Paint the ice cream stick with the metallic gold paint or marker pen and allow it to dry.

2 Wind the craft wire around a piece of gold cord and then roll the cord into a spiral. Repeat, so you have two cord spirals.

3 Cut out pieces of card, and glue the cord spirals to them. Then cut round the spirals.

4 Glue the spirals card-side down to each end of the stick.

Did you know...
Gold, silver, bronze, amber and bone were used to make fibulae.

5 Decorate the middle of the stick by winding more gold cord around it.

6 Tape the safety pin to the other side of the ice cream stick, so you can pin it on.

make a Hoplite's shield

Greek foot soldiers were called hoplites after the large shields, called hoplons, that they carried. Hoplons were made from wood, covered with bronze or leather and decorated with symbols or characters from Greek mythology.

You will need:
- ◎ Large paper plate
- ◎ Black card
- ◎ Scissors
- ◎ Red construction paper
- ◎ Glue and sticky tape
- ◎ Gold craft foil
- ◎ Glitter glue

1 Cut out a circle of black card larger than the paper plate.

2 Fold the red paper in half and cut a line of triangles along the fold, then cut along the fold. Repeat to make enough triangles to go around the edge of the circle and then glue them to the card.

3 Cover the plate with gold foil and glue it rim-side down onto the middle of the card.

4

Cut four narrow strips of red paper and glue them onto the front of the shield to form the V shape.

Did you know...
Hoplites fought with spears and swords.

5

Paint on dots of glitter glue around the V and the rim of your shield.

6

Cut a wide strip of card, fold it back at each end and glue or tape it onto the back of the shield to form a handle.

make a
Greek arm guard

Greek soldiers wore arm guards made of bronze in battle. The guards covered and protected their arms from the wrist to the elbow.

1 Draw a shape like the one in the picture onto a piece of card, and cut it out. It should be big enough to cover your forearm.

2 Bend the card to form a tube that will fit around your arm and tape the edges together.

3 For papier maché, mix up equal parts of water and white glue. Tear thin strips of tissue paper and smooth them onto the card. Continue laying on more strips of paper, making criss-cross patterns, and allow them to dry.

4 Cut some pieces of string and glue them around both edges of the tube. Glue two long pieces onto the tube to make a curved symmetrical pattern.

Did you know...
Hoplites also wore helmets, breast plates and leg guards made from bronze.

5 Look for the point where the card template was taped together and cut the tube open along this line so you can fit it around your arm.

6 Paint the arm guard using gold metallic paint and leave it to dry. Decorate with paper fastener 'studs', making sure you tape the ends down inside the arm guard.

make a
Gable decoration

The Greeks decorated the roofs and gables of buildings and grand tombs with carved sculptures called acroteria. They were made from stone, marble or painted terracotta.

1 Roll out and trim a piece of clay to make a rectangular base 12cm by 6cm and 1cm thick.

2 Roll out and cut two strips of clay 30cm by 3cm wide.

3 Curl the strips into scrolls, then press them down onto the base facing opposite ways.

4

Shape a piece of clay into a diamond and use a tool to make a groove around it. Press it down between the scrolls and fill any gaps with clay.

5

Roll out and cut seven strips of clay 10cm long by 4cm wide.

6

Make seven small balls of clay and place one in the centre of each strip. Fold each strip in half, and press onto the scrolls.

make a
Discus

Discus throwing was a popular sport at the ancient Greek Olympics. Athletes competed to see who could throw a heavy discus made from iron or bronze over the longest distance.

1 Glue the paper plates together rim to rim.

2 Paint the plates, using grey and brown paint or metallic paint to look like bronze.

3 Use the compasses to draw three concentric circles on the back of each plate. Go over the circles with marker pen.

4 Use glitter glue to go over each circle.

Did you know...
The word alphabet comes from the ancient Greek letters for A and B.

5 Use the metallic or white pen to decorate the discus. You could write letters from the Greek alphabet, as shown here.

make
Pan pipes

Pan pipes are named after the Greek god Pan. Greek mythology says that he made pipes from water reeds to play music for his lost love Syrinx. Still played in many parts of the world, pan pipes can be made from reeds, bamboo, wood and other materials.

1 Cut the first straw to measure 17.5cm long, the next 15.5cm, then cut the remaining straws 13.5, 12.5, 11, 10, 9 and 8.5cm long.

2 Take a small piece of plasticine or clay and flatten it. Press one end of each straw into it, then pull it out to plug the end of the straw. Cover the ends of each straw with tape, to stop the plasticine falling out.

3 Cover one side of a craft stick with double-sided tape. Repeat for the other stick.

4

Stick the straws to the craft stick, starting with the longest and finishing with the shortest. Leave small equal gaps between them. The open tops should be in a line just above the stick.

Did you know...
Pan pipes are one of the oldest musical instruments, dating back 6000 years.

5

Press the other stick, taped side down, on top then paint both sides and allow to dry.

6

Tie a piece of twine around the sticks to carry or hang the pan pipes. Play notes by blowing across the top of each straw.

Glossary

Bamboo A tall plant with a hollow, woody stem.

Bronze An orange-brown metal made from a mix of copper and tin.

Colony A country under the political rule of another country.

Discus A heavy disc thrown in athletics competitions.

Gable The triangular part of a wall between two roofs.

Grape vine The plant, or vine, on which grapes grow.

Linen A fabric made from a plant called flax.

Marble A hard stone that can be polished.

Mythology A collection of myths – ancient stories about gods, heroes and magical beasts.

Philosopher A great thinker.

Potter A person who makes pottery.

Pottery Pots, dishes and other objects made from baked clay.

Reed A plant with a long, thin stem that grows near water.

Sculptor A person who makes sculptures.

Sculpture A work of art that has been carved, modelled or cast in materials including stone, wood and bronze.

Seafaring Travelling by sea.

Shield A piece of armour carried by soldiers to protect themselves against weapon strikes.

Terracotta Brownish-red pottery or clay.

Tomb A small building that acts as a grave, where someone's body is put when he or she dies.

Zeus Greek god of the sky, and ruler of all the Olympian gods.

Further information

BOOKS

At Home With: The Ancient Greeks by Tim Cooke (Wayland, 2014)

Encounters with the Past: Meet the Ancient Greeks by Liz Miles (Franklin Watts, 2014)

Explore! Ancient Greeks by Jane Bingham (Wayland, 2014)

The History Detective Investigates: Ancient Greece by Rachel Minay (Wayland, 2014)

History Showtime: Ancient Greeks by Avril Thompson and Liza Phipps (Franklin Watts, 2013)

Monstrous Myths: Tales of Ancient Greece by Clare Hibbert (Franklin Watts, 2014)

What They Don't Tell You About: Ancient Greece by Bob Fowke (Wayland, 2013)

WEBSITES

http://www.bbc.co.uk/schools/primaryhistory/ancient_greeks/
This BBC website is full of great information about ancient Greece, including a timeline and a Greek Hero game, and is designed to support primary history teaching.

http://www.mythweb.com
Lots of information about gods, heroes and monsters of Greek myths.

http://www.ancientgreece.co.uk
The British Museum's website is designed specifically for Key Stage 2 history teaching.

http://www.childrensuniversity.manchester.ac.uk/interactives/history/greece/
A fun, interactive website from The University of Manchester, with a section on the Greek alphabet and language and a quiz at the end.

Index